Vegan Bulgar
to Keep Body and Soul Healthy

by **Vesela Tabakova**

Table Of Contents

Introduction

Bulgarian cuisine is a mix of South European and Mediterranean influences, and is rightly famous for its hearty, slow- cooked dishes made with fresh vegetables and herbs. Bulgarian cooking is mostly home cooking and vegan food is delicious, healthy and diet friendly.

The Eastern Orthodox religious tradition prescribes periods of four to seven weeks' fasting before Christmas and Easter during which only vegan food is to be consumed. In other words, these are periods when all those who fast in order to cleanse body and soul actually follow a vegan diet. Recently, many people have taken up fasting primarily for health reasons. Traditional Bulgarian cuisine, therefore, offers a large variety of vegan salads, soups and stews, as well as desserts, so one need never be bored.

This book does not contain an exhaustive inventory of Bulgarian vegan recipes; rather it includes my personal favorites. I have focused on dishes which are easy to prepare, tasty and healthy (for example, almost no fried foods are included). It is also worth mentioning that Bulgarian vegan stews taste even better the next day, so can be prepared in advance and left in the fridge, ready for a delicious meal on a busy day.

So, if you are feeling adventurous and would like to try something new, why not try Bulgarian vegan cuisine!

1. Salads and Appetizers

1.1. Beetroot Salad

Serves 4

Ingredients:

2-3 small beets, peeled

3 spring onions, cut

3 cloves garlic, pressed

2 tbsp red wine vinegar

2-3 tbsp sunflower oil

salt, to taste

Directions:

Place the beats in a steam basket set over a pot of boiling water. Steam for about 12-15 minutes, or until tender. Leave to cool.

Grate the beets and put them in a salad bowl. Add the crushed garlic cloves, the finely cut spring onions and mix well. Season with salt, vinegar and sunflower oil.

1.2. The Best Orzo Salad

Serves 6

Ingredients:

For the dressing:

1/3 cup extra-virgin olive oil

3/4 cup fresh lemon juice

1 tbsp dried mint

For the salad:

9 oz uncooked orzo

2 tbsp olive oil

a bunch of spring onions, chopped

½ cup chopped green peppers

½ cup stoneless black olives, cut

1 cup fresh tomatoes, diced

1 cup raw sunflower seeds

Directions:

The dressing: Combine the olive oil, lemon juice, and mint in a small bowl, mixing well. Place the dressing in the refrigerator until ready to use.

Cook the orzo according to package directions (in salted water) and rinse thoroughly with cold water when you strain it. Transfer to a large bowl and toss with the olive oil. Allow orzo to cool completely.

Once orzo is cooled, add the diced peppers, finely cut fresh onions, olives and diced tomatoes stirring until mixed well.

Stir the dressing (it will have separated by this point) and add it to the salad, tossing to evenly coat. Add salt and pepper to taste and sprinkle with sunflower seeds.

1.3. Fried Zucchinis with Tomato Sauce

Serves 4

Ingredients:

4 zucchinis medium size

1 cup all purpose flour

Salt

For the tomato sauce

4-5 ripe tomatoes, skinned and grated

1 carrot

½ onion

2 cloves garlic, whole

1 tsp salt

11/2 cup sunflower oil

1 tsp sugar

3.5 oz flour

¼ bunch fresh parsley, finely cut

Directions:

Wash and peel the zucchinis, and cut them in thin diagonal slices or in rings. Salt and leave them in a suitable bowl placing it inclined to drain away the juices.

Coat the zucchinis with flour, then fry turning on both sides until they are golden-brown (about 3 minutes on each side). Transfer to paper towels and pat dry.

Heat the oil in a large skillet and cook the onion and the carrot until soft. Add the grated tomatoes together with two whole garlic cloves. Season with salt and half a teaspoon of sugar. Simmer in low heath until thick and ready. Sprinkle with the parsley and pour over the fried zucchinis.

1.4. Couscous Salad

Serves 4

Ingredients:

9 oz couscous

1 1/2 cup hot water

2 ripe tomatoes, diced

½ red onion, finely cut

5 tbsp olive oil

3 tbsp lemon juice

1 tbsp dry mint

Directions:

Place the couscous in a large bowl. Boil water and 1 tablespoon olive oil and pour over the couscous. Cover and set aside for 10 minutes.

Fluff couscous with a fork and when it is completely cold, stir in the tomatoes, onion and dry mint.

In a separate small bowl, combine the remaining olive oil, the lemon juice and salt, add to the couscous and stir until well combined.

1.5. Green Salad

Serves 4

Ingredients:

one head of lettuce, washed and drained

1 cucumber

1 bunch of radishes

1 bunch of spring onions

the juice of half a lemon or 2 tbsp of white wine vinegar

3 tbsp sunflower or olive oil

salt, to taste

Directions:

Cut the lettuce into thin strips. Slice the cucumber and the radishes as thinly as possible and chop the spring onions.

Mix all the salad ingredients in a large bowl, add the lemon juice and oil and season with salt to taste.

1.6. Roasted Aubergines and Peppers Relish

Serves 4

Ingredients:

2 medium aubergines (eggplants)

2 red or green bell peppers

2 tomatoes

3 cloves garlic, crushed

fresh parsley

1-2 tbsp red wine vinegar

olive oil, as needed

salt and pepper, to taste

Directions:

Wash and dry the vegetables. Prick the skin of the aubergines. Bake the aubergines, tomatoes and peppers in a pre-heated oven at 420F for about 40 minutes, until the skins are pretty burnt. Take out of the oven and leave in a covered container for about 10 minutes.

Peel the skins off and drain well the extra juices. De-seed the peppers. Cut all the vegetables into small pieces. Add the garlic and mix well with a fork or in a food processor. Add the olive oil, vinegar and salt to taste. Stir again. Serve cold and sprinkled with parsley.

1.7. Potato Salad

Serves 5-6

Ingredients:

4-5 large potatoes

2-3 spring onions, finely chopped

juice of 1/2 a lemon

1/4 cup sunflower or olive oil

salt and pepper to taste

fresh parsley, finely cut

Directions:

Peel and boil the potatoes for about 20-25 minutes, drain and leave to cool.

In a salad bowl, add the finely chopped spring onions, the lemon juice, salt, pepper and olive oil, and mix gently. Cut the potatoes into cubes and add to the salad bowl. Gently mix, sprinkle with parsley. Serve cold.

1.8. Haricot Bean Salad

Serves: 4-5

Ingredients:

9 oz haricot beans

1 onion

3 tbsp white vinegar

a bunch of fresh parsley

salt and black pepper, to taste

Directions:

Wash the beans and soak them in cold water to swell overnight. Cook in the same water with the peeled onion. When tender, drain and put into a deeper bowl. Remove the onion.

Mix well oil, vinegar, salt and pepper. Pour over still warm beans, leave to cool about 30-40 minutes. Chop the onion and the parsley, add to the beans, mix and serve.

1.9. Cabbage Salad

Serves 4

Ingredients:

9 oz fresh white cabbage, shredded

9 oz carrots, shredded

9 oz white turnips, shredded

½ a bunch of parsley

2 tbsp white vinegar

3 tbsp sunflower oil

salt, to taste

Directions:

Combine first three ingredients in a large bowl - and mix well. Add the salt, vinegar and oil. Stir and sprinkle with parsley.

1.10. Roasted Peppers with Garlic and Parsley

Serves 4-6

Ingredients:

2 lb red and green bell peppers

1/2 cup sunflower oil

5-6 tbsp white vinegar

3-4 cloves garlic, chopped

a small bunch of fresh parsley

salt and pepper, to taste

Directions:

Grill the peppers or roast them in the oven at 420F until the skins are a little burnt. Place the roasted peppers in a brown paper bag or a lidded container and leave covered for about 10 minutes. This makes it easier to peel them. Peel the skins and remove the seeds.

Cut the peppers into strips lengthwise and layer them in a bowl.

Mix together the oil, vinegar, salt and pepper, chopped garlic and the chopped parsley leaves. Pour over the peppers. Cover the roasted peppers and chill for an hour.

1.11. Cucumber Salad

Serves 4

Ingredients:

2 medium cucumbers, sliced

a bunch of fresh dill

2 cloves garlic

3 tbsp white vinegar

5 tbsp olive oil

salt, to taste

Directions:

Cut the cucumbers in rings and put them in a salad bowl. Add the finely cut dill, the pressed garlic and season with salt, vinegar and oil.

Mix well and serve cold.

2. Soups

2.1. Tomato Soup

Serves 5-6

Ingredients:

5 cups chopped fresh tomatoes or 27 oz canned tomatoes, undrained

1 large onion, diced

4 garlic cloves, minced

1/4 cup white rice

1 cup water

3 tbsp olive oil

1/2 tsp salt

½ tsp black pepper

1 tsp sugar

½ bunch of fresh parsley, finely cut

Directions:

Sauté onions and garlic in oil in a large soup pot. When onions have softened, add tomatoes and cook until onions are golden and tomatoes soft. Stir in the spices and mix well to coat vegetables.

Blend the soup then return to the pot. Add the rice, the water, and a teaspoon of sugar and bring to boil, then simmer 20-30 minutes stirring occasionally. Sprinkle with parsley and serve.

2.2. Monastery Style Haricot Bean Soup

Serves 6

Ingredients:

9 oz white (haricot) beans

2-3 carrots

2 onions, finely chopped

1-2 tomatoes, grated

1 red bell pepper, chopped

4-5 springs of fresh mint and parsley

1 tsp paprika

¼ cup sunflower oil

salt, to taste

Directions:

Soak the beans in cold water for 3-4 hours, drain and discard the water. Cover the beans with cold water.

Add the oil, finely chopped carrots, onions and pepper. Bring to the boil and simmer until the beans are tender.

Add the grated tomatoes, mint, paprika and salt. Simmer for another 15 minutes. Serve sprinkled with finely chopped parsley.

2.3. Cream-less Cauliflower Soup

Serves 8

Ingredients:

¼ cup olive oil

1 large onion, finely cut

1 medium head cauliflower, chopped

2-3 garlic cloves, minced

3 cups vegetable broth

salt, to taste

fresh ground black pepper, to taste

Directions:

Heat the olive oil in a large pot over medium heat, and sauté the onion, cauliflower and garlic, Stir in the vegetable broth and bring the mixture to a boil.

Reduce heat, cover, and simmer for 40 minutes. Remove the soup from heat and blend in a blender or with a hand mixer. Season with salt and pepper.

2.4. Mushroom Soup

Serves 4

Ingredients:

1.2 lb mushrooms, peeled and chopped

1 onion, chopped

2 cloves of garlic, crushed

1 tsp thyme

2 cups vegetable broth

salt and pepper, to taste

3 tbsp olive oil

Directions:

Sauté onions and garlic in a large soup pot until transparent. Add thyme and mushrooms.

Cook for 10 minutes then add the vegetable stock and simmer for another 10-20 minuets. Blend, season and serve.

2.5. Spinach Soup

Serves 4

Ingredients:

14 oz frozen spinach

1 large onion or 4-5 spring onions

1 carrot

3-4 tbsp olive or sunflower oil

1/4 cup white rice

1-2 cloves garlic, cut

1 tsp paprika

black pepper, to taste

salt, to taste

Directions:

Heat oil in a cooking pot. Add the onion and carrot and sauté together for a few minutes, until just softened. Add chopped garlic, paprika and rice and stir for a minute.

Remove from heat. Add the spinach along with about 3 cups of hot water and season with salt and pepper. Bring back to the boil, then reduce the heat and simmer for around 30 minutes.

2.6. Nettle Soup

Serves 4

Ingredients:

1.2 lb young top shoots of nettles, well washed

3-4 tbsp sunflower oil

2 potatoes, diced small

1 bunch spring onions, coarsely chopped

1 ½ cup freshly boiled water

1 tsp salt

Directions:

Clean the young nettles, wash and cook them in slightly salted water. Drain, rinse, drain again and then chop or pass through a sieve.

Sauté the chopped spring onions and potatoes in the oil until the potatoes start to color a little. Turn off the heat, add the nettles, then gradually stir in the water. Stir well, then simmer until the potatoes are cooked through.

2.7. Lentil Soup

Serves 4

Ingredients:

1 cup brown lentils

1 onion, chopped

5-6 cloves garlic, peeled

4 medium carrots, chopped

1 medium tomato, ripe

4 tbsp olive oil

1½ tsp paprika

1 tsp summer savory

Directions:

Heat the oil in a cooking pot, add the onions and carrots and sauté until golden. Add the paprika and washed lentils with 3 cups of warm water; continue to simmer.

Chop tomatoes and add them to the soup about 15 min after the lentils have started to simmer. Add savory and the peeled garlic cloves. Let it simmer until the lentils are soft. Salt to taste.

3. Main Dishes

3.1. Green Pea Stew

Serves 5

Ingredients:

1 large can green peas or a 1 bag frozen green peas drained

5 tbsp sunflower oil

1 medium onion, finely cut

2 carrots, chopped

3 cups water

1 tsp paprika

½ bunch of fresh dill

4 cloves garlic

salt, to taste

Directions:

Sauté the finely chopped onion and carrots. Add the garlic, the paprika and the green peas and simmer with warm water for 20 minutes.

Season with salt and black pepper to taste. When ready sprinkle with the finely cut dill.

3.2. Green Pea and Mushroom Stew

Serves 4

Ingredients:

1 cup green peas (fresh or frozen)

4 large mushrooms, sliced

3 spring onions, chopped

1-2 cloves garlic

4 tbsp vegetable oil

1/2 cup water

1/2 bunch of finely chopped dill

Directions:

In a saucepan, sauté mushrooms, green onions and garlic. Add green peas and stew for 5-10 minutes until tender.

When ready sprinkle with dill. Serve warm.

3.3. Leek Stew

Serves 5-6

Ingredients:

1 lb leeks, cut

salt, to taste

fresh, ground pepper to taste

4 tbsp sunflower oil

1/2 cup vegetable broth

2 tbsp tomato paste

Directions:

Carefully clean leeks; cut off the stemmy bottoms and the dark green leaves, leave only white and light green parts. Cut leeks lengthwise in quarters, then into about 3 cm squares.

Heat oil in a heavy wide saucepan or sauté pan; add leeks, salt, pepper, and stir over low heat for 5 minutes. Add vegetable stock and bring to boil, cover and simmer over low heat, stirring often, for about 10 to 15 minutes or until leeks are tender.

Add tomato paste, raise heat to medium, uncover and let juices reduce to about half.

3.4. Potato and Leek Stew

Serves 4

Ingredients:

12 oz potatoes

2-3 leek stems cut into thick rings

5-6 tbsp olive oil

1/2 bunch of parsley

salt, to taste

Directions:

Peel the potatoes, wash them and cut them into small cubes. Slice the leeks. Put the potatoes and the leeks in a pot along with some water and the oil. The water should cover the vegetables.

Season with salt and bring to the boil then simmer until tender. Sprinkle with the finely chopped parsley.

3.5. Zucchinis and Rice

Serves 4

Ingredients:

2 lb small zucchinis, diced

1 bunch spring onions, finely chopped

5 tbsp sunflower oil

2 cups water

2 medium tomatoes, diced

1 cup rice

1 tsp salt

1 tsp paprika

1 tsp black pepper

2 ½ cups water

1 bunch fresh dill, finely cut

Directions:

Sauté green onions in oil and a little water. Cover and cook until soft. Transfer onions in a baking dish, add zucchinis, tomatoes, rice, salt, paprika, pepper and water. Mix well.

Cover with foil and bake in a preheated 350F oven for 30 minutes or until the rice is done. Sprinkle with dill and serve.

3.6. Spinach with Rice

Serves 4

Ingredients:

1.5 lb fresh spinach, washed, drained and chopped

1/2 cup rice

1 onion

1 carrot

5 tbsp olive oil

2 cups water

Directions:

Heat the oil in a large skillet and cook the onions and the carrot until soft, add the paprika and the washed and drained rice and mix well.

Add two cups of warm water stirring constantly as the rice absorbs it, and simmer for 10 more minutes.

Wash the spinach well and cut it in strips then add to the rice and cook until it wilts. Remove from the heat and season to taste.

3.7. Vegetable Stew

Serves 6

Ingredients:

3-4 potatoes, diced

2-3 tomatoes, diced

1-2 carrots, chopped

1-2 onions, finely chopped

1 zucchini, chopped

1 eggplant, chopped

1 celery rib, chopped

1/2 cup green peas, frozen

1/2 green beans, frozen

1/2 cup sunflower oil

1 bunch of parsley, finely cut

1 tsp black pepper

1 tsp salt

Directions:

Sauté the finely chopped onions, carrots and celery in a little oil. Add the green peas, the green beans, black pepper and stir well. Pour over 1 cup of water, cover and let simmer.

After 15 minutes add the diced potatoes, the zucchini, the eggplant and the tomato pieces. Transfer everything into a clay pot or casserole, sprinkle with parsley and bake for about 30 minutes at 350F.

3.8. Baked Haricot Beans

Serves 8-10

Ingredients:

1 1/2 dried white (haricot) beans

2 medium onions

1 red bell pepper, chopped

1 carrot, chopped

1/4 cup sunflower oil

1 tsp paprika

1 tsp black pepper

1 tbsp plain flour

½ bunch fresh parsley and mint

1 tsp salt

Directions:

Wash the beans and soak in water overnight. In the morning discard the water, pour enough cold water to cover the beans, add one of the onions, peeled but left whole. Cook until the beans are soft but not falling apart. If there is too much water left, drain the beans.

Chop the other onion and fry it a frying pan along with the chopped bell pepper and the carrot. Add paprika, plain flour and the beans. Stir well and pour the mixture in a baking dish along with some parsley, mint, and salt.

Bake in a preheated to 350 oven for 20-30 minutes. The beans should not be too dry. Serve warm.

3.9. Rice Stuffed Bell Peppers

Serves 4

Ingredients:

8 bell peppers, cored and seeded

11/2 cups rice

2 onions, chopped

1 tomato, chopped

fresh parsley, chopped

3 tbsp oil

1 tbsp paprika

Directions:

Heat the oil and sauté the onions for 2-3 minutes. Add the paprika, the washed and rinsed rice, the tomato, and season with salt and pepper. Add ½ cup of hot water and cook the rice until the water is absorbed.

Stuff each pepper with the mixture using a spoon. Every pepper should be ¾ full. Arrange the peppers in a deep oven proof dish and top up with warm water to half fill the dish.

Cover and bake for about 20 minutes at 350F. Uncover and cook for another 15 minutes until the peppers are well cooked.

3.10. Stuffed Red Bell Peppers with Haricot Beans

Serves 5

Ingredients:

10 dried red bell peppers

1 cup dried white beans

1 onion

3 cloves garlic, cut

2 tbsp flour

1 carrot

1 bunch of parsley

1/2 cup crushed walnuts

1 tsp paprika

salt, to taste

Directions:

Put the dried peppers in warm water and leave them for 1 hour. Cook the beans. Chop the carrot and the onion, sauté them and add them to the cooked beans. Add as well the finely chopped parsley and the walnuts. Stir the mixture to make it homogeneous.

Drain the peppers, then fill them with the mixture and place in a roasting tin, covering the peppers' openings with flour to seal them during the baking. Bake it for about 30 min at 350F.

3.11. Stuffed Grapevine Leaves – Lozovi Sarmi

Serves 6

Ingredients:

1.5 oz grapevine leaves, canned

2 cups rice

2 onions, chopped

2-3 cloves garlic, chopped

1/2 cup of currants

half bunch of parsley

half bunch of dill

1 lemon, juice only

1 tsp dried mint

1 tsp salt

1 tsp black pepper

1 cup extra virgin olive oil

Directions:

Heat 3 tablespoons of olive oil in a frying pan and sauté the onions and garlic until golden. Add the washed and drained rice, the currants, dill and parsley. Pour half a cup of olive oil and lemon juice in it. Add the black pepper, dried mint, salt and stir well.

Place leaf on a chopping board, with the stalk towards you and the vein side up. Snip away any tough remnants of the vein. Place about 1 teaspoon of the filling in the center of the leaf and towards the bottom edge. Fold the bottom part of the leaf over the filling, then draw the sides in and towards the middle, rolling the leaf up. The vine leaves should be well tucked in, forming a neat parcel. The stuffing should feel compact and evenly distributed.

Cover the bottom of a pot with grapevine leaves and stand the stuffed vine leaf parcels, packing them tightly together, on top. Pour water some water, to just below the level of the stuffed leaves. Pour ½ cup olive oil over the stuffed vine leaves, then place a small, flat oven proof dish upside down on top, in order to prevent scattering. Cover with a lid.

Bring to the boil, then reduce the heat and simmer for about an hour checking occasionally that the bottom of the pot does not burn. The liquid should be absorbed giving a lovely sticky finish to the stuffed leaves. Serve warm or cold.

3.12. Green Bean and Potato Stew

Serves 5-6

Ingredients:

2 cups green beans, fresh or frozen

2 onions, chopped

4 cloves garlic, crushed

1 cup olive oil

1 cup fresh parsley, chopped

1 bunch of fresh dill, finely chopped

3-4 potatoes, peeled and cut in small chunks

2 carrots, sliced

1/2 cup water

2 tsp tomato paste

salt and pepper, to taste

Directions:

Sauté the onions and the garlic lightly in olive oil. Add the green beans, and the remaining ingredients.

Cover and simmer over medium heat for about an hour or until all vegetables are tender. Check after 30 minutes; add more water if necessary. Serve warm - sprinkled with the fresh dill.

3.13. Cabbage and Rice Stew

Serves 4

Ingredients:

1 cup long grain white rice

2 cups water

2 tbsp olive oil

1 small onion, chopped

1 clove garlic, crushed

1/4 head cabbage, cored and shredded

2 tomatoes, diced

1 tbsp paprika

1/2 bunch of parsley

salt to taste

black pepper, to taste

Directions:

Heat the olive oil in a large pot. Add the onion and garlic and cook until transparent. Add the paprika, rice and water, stir and bring to boil.

Simmer for 10 minutes. Add the shredded cabbage, the tomatoes, and cook for about 20 minutes, stirring occasionally, until the cabbage cooks down. Season with salt and pepper and serve sprinkled with parsley.

3.14. Rice with Leeks and Olives

Serves 4-6

Ingredients:

6 large leeks, cleaned and sliced into bite sized pieces (about 6-7 cups of sliced leeks)

1 large onion, cut

20 black olives pitted, chopped

1/2 cup hot water

1/4 cup olive oil

1 cup rice

2 cups boiling water

freshly-ground black pepper, to taste

Directions:

In a large saucepan, sauté the leeks and onion in the olive oil for 4-5 minutes. Cut and add the olives and 1/2 cup water. Bring temperature down, cover saucepan and cook for 10 minutes, stirring occasionally.

Add rice and 2 cups of hot water, bring to boil, cover and simmer for 15 more minutes, stirring occasionally.

Remove from heat and allow to 'sit' for 30 minutes before serving so that the rice can absorb any liquid left.

3.15. Rice and Tomatoes

Serves 6-7

Ingredients:

1 cup rice

1 big onion, chopped

1 tbsp paprika

1/4 cup olive oil

1 tsp savory

1 large can tomatoes, diced

or 5 big ripe tomatoes

½ bunch fresh parsley, finely cut

1 tsp sugar

Directions:

Wash and drain the rice. In a large saucepan, sauté the onion in the olive oil for 4-5 minutes. Add paprika and rice stirring constantly until the rice becomes transparent.

Pour 2 cups hot water and the tomatoes. Mix well and season with salt, pepper, savory and a tsp of sugar to neutralize the acidic taste of the tomatoes.

Simmer over medium heath for about 20 minutes. When ready sprinkle with parsley.

3.16. Roasted Cauliflower

Serves 4

Ingredients:

1 medium cauliflower, cut into bite sized pieces

4 garlic cloves, lightly crushed

1 tsp fresh rosemary

salt to taste

black pepper

1/4 cup olive oil

Directions:

Mix oil, rosemary, salt, pepper and garlic together. Toss in cauliflower and place in a baking dish in one layer.

Roast in a preheated oven at 350F for 20 minutes; stir and bake for 10 more minutes.

3.17. Stuffed Cabbage Leaves – Zelevi Sarmi

Serves 8

Ingredients:

20-30 pickled cabbage leaves

1 onion, diced

2 leeks stems, chopped

1 1/2 cup white rice

1/2 cup currants

1/2 cup almonds, blanched, peeled, and chopped

2 tsp paprika

1 tbsp dried mint

1/2 tsp black pepper

½ cup olive oil

salt, to taste

Directions:

Sauté the onion and the leeks in the oil for about 2-3 minutes. Add the paprika, the black pepper and the washed and drained rice and continue Sautéing until the rice is translucent. Remove from heat and add the currants, finely chopped almonds and the peppermint. Add salt only if the cabbage leaves are not too salty.

In a large pot place a few cabbage leaves on the base. Place a cabbage leaf on a large plate with the thickest part closest to you. Spoon 1-2 teaspoons of the rice mixture and fold over each edge to create a tight sausage-like parcel. Place in the pot, making two or three layers of sarmi.

Cover with a few cabbage leaves and pour over some boiling

water so that the water level remains lower than the top layer of cabbage leaves. Top with a small dish upside down to prevent scattering. Bring to the boil then lower the heat and cook for around 40 minutes. Serve warm or at room temperature.

3.18. New Potatoes with Herbs

Serves 4-5

Ingredients:

2.25 oz small new potatoes

1 tbsp mint

5 tbsp olive oil

1 tbsp finely chopped parsley

1 tbsp rosemary

1 tbsp oregano

1 tbsp dill

1 tsp salt

1 tsp black pepper

Directions:

Wash the young potatoes, cut them in halves if too big, and put them in a baking dish. Pour the olive oil over the potatoes.

Season with the herbs, salt and pepper. Bake for 30-40 minutes at 350F.

4. Desserts

4.1. Baked Apples

Serves 4

Ingredients:

8 medium sized apples

1/3 cup walnuts, crushed

3/4 cup sugar

3 tbsp raisins, soaked

vanilla, cinnamon according to taste

Directions:

Peel and carefully hollow the apples. Prepare stuffing by mixing 3/4 cup of sugar, crushed walnuts, raisins and cinnamon.

Stuff the apples and place in an oiled dish, pour over 1-2 tbsp of water and bake in a moderate oven. Serve warm.

4.2. Pumpkin Baked with Dry Fruit

Serves 5-6

Ingredients:

1.5 lb pumpkin, cut into medium pieces

1 cup dry fruit (apricots, plums, apples, raisins)

1/2 cup brown sugar

Directions:

Soak the dry fruit in some water, drain and discard the water. Cut the pumpkin in medium cubes. At the bottom of a pot arrange a layer of pumpkin pieces, then a layer of dry fruit and then again some pumpkin.

Add a little water. Cover the pot and bring to boil. Simmer until there is no more water left. When almost ready add the sugar. Serve warm or cold.

4.3. Pumpkin Pastry

Serves 8

Ingredients:

14 oz filo pastry

14 oz pumpkin

1 cup walnuts, coarsely chopped

1/2 cup sugar

6 tbsp sunflower oil

1 tbsp cinnamon

1 tsp vanilla

Directions:

Grate the pumpkin and steam it until tender. Cool and add the walnuts, sugar, cinnamon and the vanilla.

Place a few sheets of pastry in the baking dish, sprinkle with oil and spread the filling on top. Repeat this a few times finishing with a sheet of pastry.

Bake for 20 minutes at medium heat. Let the Pumpkin Pie cool down and dust with the powdered sugar.

4.4. Apple Pastry

Serves 8

Ingredients:

14 filo pastry

5-6 apples, peeled and cut

11/2 cup walnuts, coarsely chopped

2/3 cup sugar

6 tbsp oil

1 tbsp cinnamon

1/2 tsp vanilla

Directions:

Cut the apples in small pieces and mix with the walnuts, sugar, cinnamon and the vanilla.

Place two sheets of pastry in the baking dish, sprinkle with oil and spread the filling on top. Repeat this a few times finishing with a sheet of pastry.

Bake for 20 minutes at medium heat. Let the Apple Pastry cool down and dust with the powdered sugar.

4.5. Pumpkin Cake

Serves 12

Ingredients:

2 cups grated pumpkin

11/2 cup sugar

1 tsp cinnamon

1/2 cup sunflower oil

1 cup warm water

1 cup ground walnuts

3 cups plain flour

1 tbsp baking powder

Directions:

Mix sugar and grated pumpkin with cinnamon and leave for 15 minutes to absorb the aroma. Add oil and mix well with a fork. Add warm water and the crushed walnuts stirring well. Mix well the baking powder with the flour and gently add to the dough.

Preheat oven to 350 F. Pour the dough in an oiled and floured round cake tin. Bake for about 35 minutes. When ready and cold turn over a plate and sprinkle with icing sugar.

4.6. Simple Vegan Cake

Serves 12

Ingredients:

1/2 cup sugar

1 cup fruit jam

1 cup cool water

1/2 cup vegetable oil

1 tsp vanilla powder

½ tsp cinnamon

1 cup crushed walnuts

1 tsp baking soda

21/2 cups flour

Directions:

Mix the baking soda with the jam and leave for 10 min.

Add sugar, water, oil, walnuts and flour in that order.

Mix well and pour in a round diameter cake tin. Bake in a preheated to 350F oven. When ready turn over a plate and sprinkle with powdered sugar.

About the Author

Vesela lives in Bulgaria with her family of six (including the Jack Russell Terrier). Her passion is going green in everyday life and she loves to prepare homemade cosmetic and beauty products for all her family and friends.

Vesela has been publishing her cookbooks for over a year now. If you want to see other healthy family recipes that she has published, together with some natural beauty books, you can check out her Author Page on Amazon.

Made in the USA
Middletown, DE
02 January 2020

82416016R00033